Bartnicki

Strings and Things

Strings and Things

Poems and Other Messages for Children

Christy Kenneally

Paulist Press New York/Ramsey

Art and Design: Gloria Ortíz

Library of Congress
Catalog Card Number: 84-60669

ISBN: 0-8091-6555-4

Published by Paulist Press
545 Island Road, Ramsey, N.J. 07446

Printed and bound in the
United States of America

Contents

About Growing

The child grew and became strong;
he was full of wisdom and God's
blessings were upon him.

Luke 2:40

The Seed Who Didn't Want to Grow

    Sometimes people are afraid to grow. They say, "I'm fine here by myself. I'm very cozy and comfortable staying all by myself." But being "all by myself" means being alone, and the Bible says that's not good for us. Our Father tells each one of us that we are His special children, but He reminds us that we have brothers and sisters too.

    We belong to a family and it's only when we are living and loving that we are really loving God as He would really like.

The Seed Who Didn't Want to Grow

There once was a seed
Who didn't want to grow.
He wanted to stay
In the dark down below.
And even when rain came
And tapped on his door
Saying, "Come out to play,"
He just curled up more.
His brothers and sisters were growing up fast
They said, "Hurry up, brother,
Or else you'll be last.
We can dance with the wind
And grow side by side
And drink in the rain."
But their brother replied,
"I'm not going up
To be shaken and blown
By the wind and the rain.
I'll just stay on my own."
But still they insisted:
"Come, brother, grow—
And we'll stand close together
When Winter winds blow."
So he stretched himself upwards
With all of his might,
And he burst through the earth
To the air and the light,
And he danced with the others
For many an hour,
No longer a seed
But a beautiful flower.

Moses

Some people are very big people because they have a special love for the small, quiet, anxious people. They know it isn't easy just to "Come out of your shell," so they come right in to that shell and lead you out. They aren't rough or rude or bullying. They don't mind waiting with you until you are ready to come out. We call them leaders. Moses wasn't good at making speeches. He didn't like to be in the limelight, but he led his people out of Egypt to a better life.

Moses

The evening sunlight faded from the land.
The moon was rising silvery and pale.
The young man sat in silence on the sand
And listened to the old man tell his tale.

He was afraid, he said, and ran away
To wander in the waste of desert sands.
He was an outlaw from that very day
He wore Egyptian blood upon his hands.

Then somewhere in the desert's blinding heat,
A place where desert bushes seemed to burn,
He shook the leather sandals from his feet
And heard the voice of God bid him return.

"Send Aaron, Lord," he said. "Let Aaron speak.
He speaks so well and my words stumble so.
The Pharaoh will not listen to the weak."
"Your words will come from me," God said. "Now go."

And then when God had shown His mighty hand
And through His servant Moses set them free
The people marched towards their Promised Land
Across the dried up bottom of the sea.

And though the people sometimes went astray
And at the foot of Sinai worshiped gold,
Yet Moses led them back upon the way,
The way to milk and honey, long foretold.

"And so," the old man said, "when young men meet
And ask who was the bravest one of all,
Remember well the man who bared his feet
And listened to his Master's desert call.

Though slow of speech and filled with fear and doubt,
He freed the tribe of God and led them out."

The Seasons

I remember Spring—
The dancing happy flowers,
The way the birds would sing,
And puddles after showers.

The Summer followed Spring,
With long and lazy days
To run and jump and swing
And play in many ways.

The Autumn came too soon
And all the leaves turned brown.
I walked between the trees
And watched them falling down.

The Winter came at last
And snow was all around.
But deep beneath the snow
The buds grew underground,
And to the little buds
God sends the drops of rain
To knock upon the ground
And call them up again.

The Beauty of Spring

The little daisy curled up tight
Will wake up when the sun is bright
And call to all the daisies near:
"Oh wake up, brothers. Spring is here."

Oh look, the daffodils so tall
Are nodding there beside the wall,
And look, the grass so long and green—
The greenest grass we've ever seen.

Oh look, the buds on every tree,
And hear the busy busy bee.
Oh look at every growing thing.
We thank you, thank you, God,
For Spring.

The Butterfly

Does love ever end? No. The Bible says, All other things may end but love can't because God is love. But surely death ends love? No again. Death just changes love, as all the little garden creatures discover.

The Butterfly

A spider spun a silken thread
And swung from grass to ground.
"I must find out the news," he said,
"That's buzzing all around."
The garden creatures big and small
Were quiet as a mouse.
They saw the caterpillar crawl
Into a tiny house.

"He's such a fool," said the ladybird,
As she polished up her nails.
"It's the silliest thing we've ever heard,"
Said a pair of solemn snails.
So all the creatures went away,
All thinking he was dead,
Until one bright and lovely day
A little earthworm said,
"I see a crack in the little shell,
And someone moves inside.

I see a head and wings as well.
Come quick and see," he cried.
"The caterpillar's back," they said.
Before their very eyes
A butterfly stepped out instead
And smiled at their surprise.
"I left the life and friends I knew.
You thought that I was dead.
I did it just to prove to you
We die to grow," he said.

About Creating

In the beginning God created the universe. . . .
God looked on everything he had made, and
he was very pleased.

Genesis 1:1, 31

19

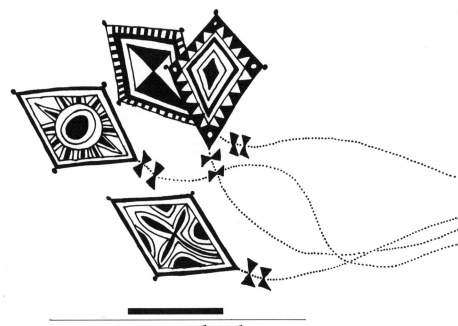

Strings and Things

Did you ever sit on a beach building a fort with high sandy walls, a bridge you could see under, and maybe a moat you could fill with buckets of sea water?

You had an idea that went from your head to your hands, and there it was.

God wasn't mean when He made us. He gave us the greatest gift of all—the gift of being able to make or create. Every time we draw something or build something, or write something, we are saying "Thank you" to God for that gift.

Many people have special gifts, but everyone has one gift—the gift of making friends, of caring for someone else. This is the most important of all the gifts. It's called Love.

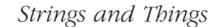

Strings and Things

Yesterday I took some twine
And with two cans I made a line,
Then with my friend from down the road
Sent messages in secret code.

With lollipop sticks we made a raft;
We made a speech and launched our craft
To sail upon a muddy sea
Created by my friend and me.

We've dug canals from pool to pool.
We've learned to draw and paint in school.
We've built a kite that really flew.
If we could do it, so could you.

A sharpened stone, a piece of slate
Are paints and easel to create
A gull with long and chalky wings.
We can create such lovely things.

Creation

All the good stories begin at "Once upon a time," but the "Best Story" begins "In the beginning." The Creation Story is as powerful as the great wave that makes the beach tremble, and as gentle as the dewdrop slowly slipping down a shiny leaf.

It is the story of the elephant and the ant, the mighty eagle and the lilting lark.

You'll find it in the Book of Genesis, right at the beginning of your Bible. It's a beautiful beginning to a beautiful story—the Love Story about God and His People.

The Creation Story reminds us that beautiful things like nodding flowers, huge iceberg clouds, or tiny dewdrops in a spider's web are especially beautiful when we can share them with somebody.

Creation

Long ago, long long ago,
When all was darkness deep and low
The voice of God called forth the light
To split the curtain of the night.
Then what was light He called the day
While what was night in darkness lay.

Then God divided earth and sea
And marked the place where each should be,
With mountains rising high and steep
And oceans spreading wide and deep.

Then God called seeds to sprout and grow
And all the flowers that we know.
The trees and grass both great and small
All blossomed when they heard His call.

Then God said, "Let the darkest night
Be filled with tiny glowing lights."
He called the sun to light the day,
The moon to keep the dark away.

Then God called all that swim and fly.
The creatures of the sea and sky,
And all the creatures of the land,
Were shaped and formed by God's good hand.

When all was done God loved it all—
The dewdrop and the waterfall,
The timid creatures and the strong,
The robin and the thrush's song.

He searched the sea and sky above
To find one who would share His love.
When none was found His plan unfurled.
God made a man to share His world.
He made a man and woman too
To share His world so bright and new,
To love the earth, the sea and sky,
The creatures, fish and birds that fly.
God gave them all to man to show
His special love, long long ago.

About Friendship

And Jesus concluded, "In your opinion, which one of these three acted like a neighbor toward the man attacked by the robbers?"

The teacher of the Law answered, "The one who was kind to him."

Jesus replied, "You go, then, and do the same."

Luke 10:36–37

The Good Samaritan

Because God gives us such a wonderful talent for friendship, we must never again just "mind our own business." What happens to another is part of our business even when we don't know that other person very well. Somebody said strangers are friends who haven't met yet. Jesus told a lovely story of a stranger who couldn't mind his own business.

The Good Samaritan

A man was going on a trip,
Going to the town.
He went down to the stables
And he took the harness down.

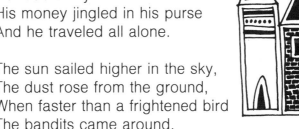

He saddled up and off he rode.
He rode away from home.
His money jingled in his purse
And he traveled all alone.

The sun sailed higher in the sky,
The dust rose from the ground,
When faster than a frightened bird
The bandits came around.

29

He tried to run, to cry for help,
He turned his mule about.
But no one came to rescue him
And no one heard his shout.

They took his purse, and took his mules.
They beat him on the head.
They galloped off with all he had
And left him there half dead.

A man was passing on that road.
He passed there every day.
He saw the traveler in the dust
And turned his head away.

"I'd stop to help that man," he said.
"I think it is a shame.
But someone else will come along,
So it's really all the same!"

Another saw him there and said,
"I think it is a crime.
I'd stop to help this wounded man
But I simply haven't time!"

Many others saw him there
And quickly hurried by,
But a stranger from another land
Took pity on his cry.

He took him to the nearest inn
And paid the landlord there
To bandage all the wounds he had
And give him every care.

The traveler asked the stranger,
"Why pay for wine and bread
For someone you have never known?"
The stranger smiled and said,

"A man who helps a weaker man
Is doing something small
For God who gave him all his strength,
For God who made us all."

The traveler took the stranger's hand.
He raised his wounded head.
"Through all the pain I've had this day
I've learned a truth," he said.

"Though you and I were strangers once,
Not speaking to each other,
You cared when others walked away,
So now I call you brother."

And so the truth the traveler learned
Is true for me and you.
Our Father made us brothers,
Not Samaritan or Jew.

The Lost Sheep

Finding a friend is wonderful. But finding means searching. We can't just sit at home waiting for a friend to call on the phone or come over.

Jesus didn't stay long in any one place. He was always searching for friends. He found them in boats, in markets and even in trees.

He made a special search for people, especially those whom nobody seemed to want to find.

The Lost Sheep

Now Jacob had a hundred sheep.
They pastured where the grass was deep.
They chewed the daylight hours away
And at night in the fold they'd stay.
But one small sheep stepped out of line.
He left the other ninety-nine.
While Jacob looked the other way
Just this one little sheep did stray.

His brothers cried, "O brother dear,
You'll come to hurt and harm we fear.
The cliffs are steep and you are small.
O we fear, brother, you may fall."

Their brother never looked behind,
Pretending he just didn't mind.
He'd do the things he wanted to,
So he just disappeared from view.

His head was full of plans and schemes.
He'd climb the hills and swim the streams.
He did not see the cliff-edge go
Till he fell to the ledge below.

When Jacob found that one was lost
He did not wait to count the cost.
He left the many safe and sound
And he searched till the one was found.

He brought him home and made him well.
His friends and neighbors made him tell
His story when his sheep was fed.
 "I've found the sheep I lost," he said.

33

My Friend

If you had one wish, what would you wish for? Think carefully now.

Remember, new clothes become old clothes, money must be spent, and nothing really lasts very long. I said "no-thing," not "no person."

The greatest gift of all is a faithful friend. Jesus is the best friend, and Jesus is in the best friends each of us have.

My Friend

There's someone very dear to me,
Almost like my family.
This someone can be he or she.
Who is it?
My friend.

There's someone knows me good and bad,
Who loves me happy, loves me sad,
The closest one I ever had.
Who is it?
My friend.

There's someone I meet every day,
Who comes to talk, who comes to play.
I'm sad when someone goes away.
Who is it?
My friend.

There's someone else I know who grew.
That someone had His own friends too.
And now He's friends with me and you.
He's Jesus, my Friend.

About Love

"Teacher, what must I do to receive eternal life?"

Jesus answered him, "What do the Scriptures say? How do you interpret them?"

The man answered, " 'Love the Lord your God with all your heart, with all your soul, and with all your strength, and with all your mind' and 'Love your neighbor as you love yourself.' "

"You are right," Jesus replied; "do this and you will live."

Luke 10:25–28

The Woman Who Found Love

Imagine love as a word you can catch very very gently like a butterfly in your hand. Imagine a poor woman who searches everywhere for it, but when she runs up to people and says, "Look, I've found love," they look in her empty hands and laugh at her. Soon their cruel laughing drives her away.

Jesus found a woman like that once. Others wanted to hurt her because she couldn't find love. Jesus looked into her heart and said, "Ah yes, I see it. Love is not in the catching and holding, but in the searching." That was a wonderful day for her. She looked into His eyes and found love. She looked at children and flowers and the sun floating in the blue lake of the sky and said, "Ah yes, *there* is love, and there and there and there. I've found it at last."

The Woman Who Found Love

The crowd had overflowed the narrow street
And flooded round the cobbled village square,
The place where holy rabbis take their seat
To teach, or lead the people in their prayer.
The Rabbi saw them throw her to the ground.
He read the shameful story in her eye.
He stood and swept His piercing gaze around
The angry mob who'd come to watch her die.

"The One who made the loving hearts of men
Knows well the loving heart will sometimes stray.
He sees the love, and so will not condemn
The heart He sees before Him here today.
If there is one of you who has no shame
Then let him throw a stone." Their hands were still.
"If one of you is pure and without blame,
If such a one is here, then let him kill."

But no hand threw and every eye looked in,
For every heart had secrets of its own,
Some shameful deed, some selfishness or sin,
And very soon the two were left alone.
She changed her life completely, people say,
And all who saw the change still praise the name
Of one who came and went upon His way,
Of one who saw her love and not her shame.

The Woman at the Well

Some people don't want other people to know who they are or what they are like. One woman who met Jesus pretended to be someone else. It was just as if she were putting on masks when Jesus spoke to her at the well.

Jesus took her masks away one by one. When he got to the true and real person she was able to recognize who Jesus was. She went out and eagerly told her neighbors about the wonderful friend she had made. Some people hide themselves because they are ashamed or afraid. They think others won't like them just as they are. Jesus was patient with people like that and gave them a new idea of how important they really are.

The Woman at the Well

The sun was hot and rosy red
And burned my garden brown.
I brought the water on my head.
The flowers drank it down.

I sat beside the village well
And watched Him as He came.
I listened to the stranger tell
The story of my shame.

"I have a special well," He said,
"A well from God above,
To raise the heart that's dry and dead
And help it grow in love."

I went from door to door that day
And brought all those in pain
To drink His words and hear Him say
How they might love again.

He left to help the lame and blind,
To comfort those who cry.
He left a well of love behind,
A well that won't run dry.

The Father Loves You Best of All

Isn't it wonderful when somebody thinks you are wonderful?

Isn't it wonderful to look at all the marvels in the world like daffodils nodding wisely on the lawn, and swallows swooping down the Summer sky, and be able to say, "In God's eyes I am worth much more than all of these."

The great thing about God's love is that there is plenty of it. Because He loves me so much doesn't mean He loves someone else less.

No. He loves me to love you.

The Father Loves You Best of All

The birds who flutter in the trees,
Who soar and hover in the sky,
Who never labor in the fields,
Who never sell and never buy,
The Father sees each tiny sparrow,
Knows each blackbird's morning call.
He knows and loves them,

One and all.
But you, his child, he loves much more
Than smallest wren or eagle strong.

Your voice is sweeter to his ear
Than any songbird's sweetest song,
He loves you more than all the earth,
And all its creatures great and small.
The Father loves you best of all.

The flowers dancing in the breeze,
The flowers peeping through the snow,
Can wear their colors as they please.
They never weave and never sow.
The Father cares for every lily,
Catches all the leaves that fall.
He clothes and keeps them one and all.
But you, his child, he loves much more
Than any flower tall and fair.
He sees you growing straight and strong.
He knows the color of your hair.
He loves you more than all the flowers,
All the forests green and tall.
The Father loves you best of all.

To every creature on the land,
Beneath the sea or in the sky,
To every seedling in the sand,
To every oak tree rising high,
To every raindrop on the window,
Every mighty waterfall,
He gives his love to one and all.
But you, his child, he loves much more
Than all the creatures on the earth.
For you he holds a special love.
For you he brought his Son to birth,
To be beside you through your life,
To catch and show you if you fall,
The Father loves you best of all.

Jesus' Birthday

Mary, will you take this baby boy?
Mary, will you take this baby boy?
Will you fill the world with love and joy?
Will you take this baby boy?

Mary, will you go to the little town?
Mary, will you go to the little town?
Will you find a manger to lay Him down?
Will you go to the little town?

Mary, will you show your little Son?
Mary, will you show your little Son?
To the kings on whom the star has shone
Will you show your little Son?

Mary, will you tell Him we love Him so?
Mary, will you tell Him we love Him so?
Will you tell Him we will shine like the star to show
That we love Him, love Him so?

Write your own poem.

Write your own poem.

Write your own poem.